Startup Secrets Unveiled:

A Guide to Launching Your Dream Business

Author

Ashley Scott

DISCLAIMER:

"Startup Secrets Unveiled: A Guide to Launching Your Dream Business", is intended as general guidance and educational purposes only and cannot guarantee complete accuracy or applicability of its information presented. Readers should exercise their own discretion before making decisions based on this book; neither the author nor publisher can be held liable for any direct or indirect damages or losses associated with its use.

AUTHORS BIO:

Ashley Scott is an experienced entrepreneur and business strategist with extensive knowledge of the startup ecosystem. Leveraging years of experience creating successful businesses, Ashley Scott brings invaluable expertise and practical insight into the writing. Their passion for entrepreneurship and commitment to helping others achieve success has made them the go-to advisor and mentor for numerous aspiring entrepreneurs. Through their book "Startup Secrets Unveiled," Ashley Scott offers readers valuable strategies, real-life examples and actionable advice to assist in their entrepreneurial journey. Focusing on practicality while having an innate desire to help others flourish, Ashley Scott strives to unlock full potential within readers while building successful businesses that leave a lasting impact.

Table Of Content

INTRODUCTION:

Welcome to "Startup Secrets Unveiled: A Guide to Launching Your Dream Business", an invaluable resource designed to arm aspiring entrepreneurs like you with all of the knowledge, strategies, and tools necessary for successfully entering and navigating the vibrant startup scene.

Build a thriving startup is an incredible journey that demands passion, creativity, resilience and strategic thinking. Each decision or action taken may have significant ramifications on its trajectory for your business.

"Startup Secrets Unveiled" offers an abundance of insights, practical advice and real-life examples from industry experts and successful entrepreneurs who have experienced the startup rollercoaster first-hand. Our aim is to give you a roadmap that will take you from sparking an idea all the way through to scaling and planning long-term success for your entrepreneurship venture.

Through these pages, you will discover the secrets to successfully navigating the startup environment. We will cover topics like ideation, market research, funding sourcing strategies, building strong teams with effective marketing and branding skills, scaling strategies for future expansion as well as planning ahead for challenges that might arise along the way.

Each chapter in this guide provides actionable strategies and frameworks you can apply directly to your own startup. We have provided real-life examples, case studies, and engaging exercises designed to encourage you to explore your ideas further, conduct market research, evaluate feasibility using tools provided, and ultimately start building.

Be mindful that every startup journey is distinct; no single approach to success exists. By drawing upon the experiences and insights shared herein, however, you will become better prepared to make informed decisions, navigate challenges with confidence, and take advantage of opportunities for growth.

No matter where your entrepreneurial journey lies, "Startup Secrets Unveiled" can serve as your trusted companion throughout it all. So grab a pen, buckle up and prepare to unlock the secrets to launching your ideal business - your entrepreneurial journey awaits!

Chapter One - Introducing Entrepreneurial Thinking

Introduction:

This chapter's introduction sets the scene by emphasizing the critical role that mindset has on entrepreneurial success. It highlights some of the unique challenges and opportunities entrepreneurs encounter as well as why cultivating the appropriate mindset can make a meaningful difference in outcomes. Furthermore, this introduction gives an overview of chapter topics including key traits analysis, risk taking strategies and resilience issues.

Section I: Recognizing the Characteristics and Attributes of Successful Entrepreneurs

1.1 Traits such as resilience, adaptability, creativity and passion:

Successful entrepreneurs possess a distinct set of traits that enable their success, like Elon Musk, the visionary behind Tesla and SpaceX. His resilience was evident as he overcame numerous setbacks and challenges during development of electric vehicles and space exploration; his adaptability demonstrated by being able to pivot strategies based on market demands; while his creativity revolutionized industries. Furthermore, Musk's passion for sustainable energy and space exploration fuels his drive to leave a positive imprint on humanity.

Exercise: Take an introspective approach to your entrepreneurial journey and identify which traits align with successful entrepreneurs. How can you further cultivate and expand these attributes to propel your venture?

1.2 Fostering a Growth Mindset and Learning from Failures:

Adopting a growth mindset is central to entrepreneurial success, as demonstrated by Sara Blakely, founder of Spanx. She kept faith with herself that she could learn and adapt while viewing failure as opportunities to hone products and business strategies - her growth mindset being instrumental in the journey that lead to creating a multi-billion-dollar company.

Case Study: Conduct research and study the journey of an accomplished entrepreneur who displays a growth mindset. Investigate their mindset shifts, how they took failure as learning opportunities and the results for their success.

Section 2: Conquering fear and taking calculated risks

2.1 Strategies for Managing and Mitigating Risk: Risk mitigation is integral to entrepreneurial success. Brian Chesky, co-founder of Airbnb, put this principle into action when faced with funding challenges; when they formulated creative ways of raising funds they decided on limited edition cereal boxes named "Obama O's" and "Cap'n McCain's", creating limited edition varieties called Obama O's" and Cap'n McCain's to generate funds while managing financial risks while building buzz around their brand - all while mitigating risks successfully and catapulting Airbnb to global hospitality disruptor.

Exercise: Recognize potential risks related to your business idea and devise plans to manage and mitigate them using Chesky as an example.

Entrepreneurs must learn to accept uncertainty and ambiguity. Sarah Leary, co-founder of Nextdoor, faced this challenge when she launched the neighborhood social networking platform. To combat any possible uncertainties regarding user adoption or engagement with Nextdoor's product offering, Leary conducted extensive user research, collected feedback from users and iterated according to user needs. By accepting uncertainty while actively involving their community in development of Nextdoor as a community platform.

Case Study: Examine the journey of a startup which successfully navigated uncertainty and ambiguity. Uncover their strategies to gather feedback, refine their product iterations process and retain user engagement.

Section 3: Fostering Resilience and Perseverance

Resilience is a key quality for successful entrepreneurs, such as Jack Ma, the co-founder of Alibaba Group. Though he faced rejections and failures on his journey to success, Ma was able to overcome setbacks through strong belief in himself and perseverance - this mental strength played an instrumental role in Alibaba becoming one of the world's largest e-commerce platforms.

Exercise: Reflect upon an experience wherein you encountered setback or failure and discuss how you managed to recover and what lessons were taken away from that experience.

Maintain Motivation and Focus:
Motivation and focus are an integral component of entrepreneurial journey. Take Oprah Winfrey for instance - she built an empire from her talk show and media network alone by using visual representation of aspirationsal goals on a vision board practice to keep herself on the journey even

through challenging times, using reminders and affirmations techniques to promote an abundance mindset that led her on an incredible success path.

Exercise: Create your own visual reminders or vision board of entrepreneurial goals, sharing key components that will keep you focused and on track on the journey ahead.

Conclusion:

In this chapter, we examined the significance of an entrepreneurial mindset for success. By drawing upon real-world examples, case studies, and exercises illustrating successful entrepreneurs' characteristics and behaviors we encouraged you to reflect upon your journey, identify unique traits within yourself, and cultivate a mindset required for entrepreneurial pursuits. By understanding successful entrepreneurs' mentalities as well as taking up exercises to practice the necessary mindset you are equipped with the resilience, risk management strategies, and motivational tools necessary for taking steps on an entrepreneurial journey.

Chapter 2: Generating Ideas and Analyzing Options

Introduction:

Every successful entrepreneur starts with a spark of an idea. In this chapter, we delve into the fascinating world of ideation and opportunity evaluation - covering techniques for creating business ideas, assessing market opportunities and conducting feasibility analyses. By adopting an organized method for ideation and evaluation, entrepreneurs can increase their odds of recognizing viable and promising opportunities.

Section I: Generating Business Ideas

Creativity is at the core of business idea generation. This section introduces various techniques entrepreneurs can employ to stimulate their creative thinking, such as brainstorming sessions, mind mapping exercises and the "SCAMPER" technique

(Substitute, Combine, Adapt Modify Put to Another Use Eliminate Reverse). We also explore "design thinking" as an avenue to discover innovative concepts.

Exercise: Schedule dedicated time for idea generation and brainstorming/mind mapping techniques to generate potential business ideas. Set yourself the goal of coming up with at least ten creative solutions by pushing yourself beyond your comfort zone.

Entrepreneurs find motivation from tapping into personal interests and passions. This section encourages readers to identify their personal areas of expertise and passions, exploring how these interests could translate to viable business opportunities. We showcase real-life examples of successful businesses which were founded based on founders' personal passions or experiences; by aligning work with passions, entrepreneurs can stay motivated on the journey while enjoying it along the way.

Case Study: Investigate and explore an already successful business founded upon its founder's personal passions or interests, and study how their passions affected its business idea, customer engagement strategy and overall success.

Section 2: Evaluating Market Opportunities

Conducting Market Research:

Market research is an integral component of business evaluation. In this section we offer guidance for conducting effective market research using different methodologies such as surveys, interviews, focus groups and secondary research to gain insights into target markets. Furthermore, the importance of collecting data, analyzing market trends and understanding customer needs and preferences are highlighted here.

Exercise: Conduct primary market research by creating a survey or interview guide and collecting feedback from your target audience. Analyze the results to identify market trends, pain points, and any possible opportunities related to your business concept.

2.2 Recognizing Customer Pain Points and Unmet Needs: Entrepreneurs understand that customer pain points and unmet needs present opportunities for innovation and business creation. In this section we look into techniques such as empathy mapping, customer journey mapping, observational research and ethnography as ways of getting an insight into customers' challenges and desires. Furthermore we stress the importance of listening actively to customers, conducting user testing sessions and using customer feedback effectively in creating products or services which effectively meet these requirements.

Case Study: Analyze a business that successfully identified and addressed customer pain points or unmet needs by conducting customer research, iterating products or services, and positioning themselves strategically in the market.

Section 3: Conduct Feasibility Studies and Evaluate Opportunities

Before embarking on any idea, entrepreneurs must carefully evaluate its feasibility and viability. In this section, we discuss all components of a feasibility study such as market analysis, technical feasibility, financial projections and operational considerations. Furthermore, we offer frameworks and templates that entrepreneurs can use to assess market size, competitive landscape requirements, resource requirements scalability risks.

Exercise: Prepare a feasibility study of your business idea by following the provided template or framework. Conduct an in-depth market analysis, assess financial projections, evaluate technical and operational feasibility as well as potential risks and devise mitigation strategies.

3.2 SWOT Analysis and Opportunity Assessment:

SWOT (Strengths, Weaknesses, Opportunities, and Threats) analysis is an invaluable way to assess opportunities. In this section, we offer guidance to entrepreneurs looking for business ideas on conducting a comprehensive SWOT analysis that assesses all four elements - strengths, weaknesses, opportunities and threats - of their venture idea. Incorporating such analysis can assist entrepreneurs with making more informed decisions and revising business strategies more efficiently.

Exercise: Conduct a SWOT analysis for your business idea. Determine its internal strengths and weaknesses, external opportunities and threats within its market space, then devise strategies to accentuate your strengths while minimizing weaknesses, seizing opportunities and mitigating threats.

Conclusion:

This chapter focused on the essential stages of ideation and opportunity evaluation, using real-life examples, case studies, exercises and tools/frameworks available to entrepreneurs for creating creative ideas, conducting market research and assessing feasibility. Readers were encouraged to participate in exercises provided, explore their own entrepreneurial concepts further while applying tools/frameworks provided to refine them further. Our next chapter will delve deeper into this topic of creating an actionable business plan to translate their concepts into tangible plans.

Chapter 3: Craft a Strong Business Plan

Introduction:

A strategic business plan serves as the cornerstone of entrepreneurial success. In this chapter, we'll examine its essential components - crafting a compelling vision, setting business objectives and strategies, creating financial projections - so you're well equipped to communicate your vision effectively and steer your venture toward its desired goals.

Section I: Generating an Engaging Vision Statement

1.1.1 Establishing the Long-term Vision and Purpose of Your Business: A clear and compelling vision forms the cornerstone of any successful business plan. In this section, we explore how entrepreneurs like Jeff Bezos (founder of Amazon), articulate their long-term vision. We examine why aligning it with personal values and goals is so essential in inspiring stakeholders, employees, and potential investors.

Exercise: Assess your entrepreneurial vision. Outline a long-term vision for your business that encompasses impactful goals and core values you hold dear. Create a statement which captures both aspirational as well as inspirational aspects.

Successful entrepreneurs typically connect their business visions with personal values and goals, often doing so to achieve long-term success. We take a look at real world examples of entrepreneurs whose businesses reflect their passions and beliefs - creating meaningful, authentic ventures that resonate with target audiences by aligning vision with values.

Case Study: Examine a business which successfully aligned its vision with its founder's personal values and goals, then explore how this alignment has affected branding, customer relations, and long-term sustainability.

Section 2: Establishing Business Objectives and Strategies

Setting Specific, Measurable, Attainable Relevant and Time-bound (SMART) goals is integral to effective business planning. In this section, we provide advice for setting SMART goals in different aspects of your business such as marketing, operations, finance and growth. We examine real-life examples of entrepreneurs who set ambitious yet attainable goals to propel their companies forward.

Exercise: Set SMART goals for each area of your business, including revenue targets, customer acquisition, product development or market expansion. Be sure to ensure they are specific, measurable, attainable, relevant and time-bound!

2.2: Generating Strategies for Marketing, Operations, Finance, and Growth:

Successful entrepreneurs create strategies to achieve their business objectives. In this section we cover key components of business strategies - marketing strategies, operations strategies, finance strategies and growth strategies - along with frameworks and tools for creating effective plans in each area. Real world examples provide insight into how entrepreneurs have used effective strategies to gain a competitive edge.

Exercise: Create a strategic plan for one key area of your business, such as marketing or operations. Utilize frameworks and tools provided to outline this strategy - target audiences, marketing channels, operational processes or financial management may all come into play when developing this strategy.

Section 3: Craft a Comprehensive Business Plan

3.1 Outlining Your Company Structure, Products or Services and Target Market:
A comprehensive business plan should provide an in-depth snapshot of your organization, products and services offered, target market and objectives. This section assists in crafting concise yet informative sections for your plan; real world

examples of successful plans will serve to demonstrate effective presentation and organization techniques.

Exercise: Create an outline for your business plan, with sections dedicated to business structure, product or service description and target market analysis. Collect relevant information and insights for each section before filling it out with content.

Financial Projections and Risk Analysis:
A key element of any business plan, financial projections and risk analysis are essential elements. In this section, we cover how to construct financial projections (revenue forecasts, expense estimates and cash flow projections). Furthermore, we explore techniques for conducting a risk analysis that identifys potential threats as well as creating risk mitigation strategies - with real world examples showing how entrepreneurs have addressed financial and operational risks when creating their plans.

Exercise: Create financial projections for your business, such as revenue forecasts, expense estimates and cash flow projections. Conduct a risk analysis, identifying potential threats and developing mitigation strategies.

Conclusion: In this chapter, we have explored the steps involved in crafting an effective business plan. By means of real-life examples and case studies as well as exercises, we emphasized the significance of crafting a compelling vision, setting SMART goals, and devising strategies. Readers were invited to actively engage with exercises as well as explore their own ideas while applying tools and frameworks provided to create their own comprehensive business plans. The next chapter will address funding and financing, providing strategies and insights into securing necessary resources for your startup venture.

Chapter 4 : Funding and Financing Strategies

Securing funding is an integral component of realizing your entrepreneurial dreams, so in this chapter we explore different funding and financing strategies that can assist with starting and growing a startup. From bootstrapping to venture capital funding, we'll explore different funding avenues while giving advice on how to approach investors. By understanding the landscape of funding available and creating a comprehensive financing plan for your venture, you can give it the financial resources it requires for growth and expansion.

Bootstrapping and Self-Funding Strategies

Bootstrapping Techniques:

Bootstrapping is an increasingly common strategy among startups in their early stages. In this section, we explore strategies for bootstrapping such as using personal savings or existing assets to generate revenue from initial customers, and real world examples of successful bootstrapped ventures to show how entrepreneurs have used innovative resource management to successfully fund their ventures.

Case Study: Conduct a case study analysis on a successful bootstrapped startup to gain an insight into its strategies used to fund growth without external investment. Focus on their financial management practices, prioritization and revenue generation processes.

Self-Funding and Personal Networks: Its Entrepreneurs often rely on themselves and personal networks as sources of initial capital for their venture. In this section we highlight the significance of tapping family, friends and personal networks for financial support; specifically emphasizing clear communication, transparency and professionalism when approaching personal connections for investments.

Exercise: Evaluate both your personal financial resources and network. Determine how much capital is self-fundable; identify potential investors within your network that may be interested in investing in your startup; create a plan to approach them professionally with this investment opportunity.

Section 2: External Funding Sources

2.1 Angel Investors and Crowdfunding:

Angel investors and crowdfunding platforms can provide startups with important sources of external funding. In this section, we explore how best to approach angel investors and present your business idea successfully; including guidance on pitch deck preparation, conducting due diligence reviews, and negotiating investment terms. Furthermore, we discuss crowdfunding platforms as a potential means of raising capital while engaging early adopters.

Case Study: Research the approach taken by a startup that successfully attracted funding through angel investors or crowdfunding campaigns, such as their pitch deck, investor communications and strategies to attract backers or investors.

2.2 Venture Capital Funding:

Venture capital funding (VC) is a popular financing solution for startups with high growth potential. This section explores the world of venture capital investment, providing insights on how to secure it. We cover topics like developing an attractive business model, demonstrating traction and scaling ability, aligning with investment thesis of VC firms, as well as real-life examples from companies who have secured funding with them.

Exercise: Create a pitch deck tailored to attracting venture capital investors for your startup, with the purpose of drawing them in as investors. Make the presentation compelling while outlining the business model, key traction metrics and growth potential.

Section 3: Grants, Loans, and Government Programs

Grants and Subsidies for Startups:

Grants and subsidies provide non-dilute sources of funding for startups. This section explores various grant opportunities from government programs that support entrepreneurship and innovation as well as guidance for finding relevant grants, writing grant proposals, and meeting application requirements.

Exercise: Conduct research and identify grants or government programs relevant to your industry or sector. Make a list of requirements, and devise a strategy for applying for appropriate grants.

3.2 Assessing Loan Options and Alternative Financing:

Loans and alternative financing solutions provide startups with capital they need for growth. In this section we discuss various loan types including small business loans, microloans and peer-to-peer lending - along with their respective advantages and considerations; providing insights on how to evaluate loan terms and assess repayment possibilities.

Case Study: Consider an instance in which a startup utilized loans or alternative financing options effectively to support their expansion. Consider their terms of the loan or arrangement, the impact it had on their finances, and any strategies used by them for managing repayments.

Conclusion: In this chapter, we explored various funding and financing strategies for startups. Through real-life examples, case studies, and exercises, we stressed the significance of bootstrapping, self-funding, and investigating external funding sources as viable options. Readers were invited to actively engage in exercises designed to assess their own funding needs before creating a comprehensive financing plan tailored specifically to their growth trajectory. Our next chapter will focus on building strong teams composed of top talent while creating an environment of innovation.

Chapter 5 : Build A Competent Team And Encourage Innovation

Building a strong team and cultivating a conducive environment to innovation are keys to any startup's success. In this chapter, we explore strategies for recruiting top talent, creating collaborative work environments, and encouraging innovation within your startup. By gathering the ideal team together and cultivating an environment conducive to creativity and innovation, your startup could reach new heights of success.

Attracting and Retaining Top Talent

1.1: Establishing the Skills and Roles Needed: Knowing which skills and roles your startup requires for creating a cohesive team is crucial to its success. In this section, we help you to define key positions and responsibilities based on your business needs and explore real-life examples of successful startups' hiring strategies that align talent with the vision and values of their companies.

Exercise: Assess and identify the key roles required within your startup business, creating job descriptions outlining each role's qualifications, skillset and responsibilities.

Recruitment and Hiring Practices for Startups:
Hiring top talent is essential to any successful startup's growth. In this section we share insight on successful recruitment strategies such as job postings, networking events, leveraging online platforms, as well as conducting in-depth interviews that assess cultural fit as well as an individual's potential contribution towards your startup's development.

Case Study: Investigate an innovative startup renowned for its exceptional hiring practices. Examine their recruitment approach, interview techniques and strategies for attracting top talent.

Section 2: Establish a Collaborative Work Environment

Fostering Teamwork and Collaboration: A collaborative work environment is key for increasing team productivity and innovation, so this section explores strategies for encouraging teamwork and collaboration within your startup. We discuss open communication, cross-functional collaboration and creating an inclusive culture which recognizes different viewpoints.

Exercise: Create and implement team-building activities or exercises within your startup to promote collaboration and problem-solving among its employees, strengthening teamwork with regular events like these.

Effective communication and feedback mechanisms: Effective and clear communication are fundamental for any thriving startup. In this section, we cover the importance of transparent channels, team meetings, and feedback mechanisms - as well as providing guidance on conducting performance reviews, providing constructive criticism, and creating an environment of continuous improvement.

Exercise: Implement a feedback mechanism within your startup, such as regular one-on-one meetings or performance reviews, that facilitates feedback delivery in an environment in which feedback is valued and accepted. Practice providing constructive advice while cultivating an environment where feedback is valued.

Section 3: Fostering Innovation Culture

Fostering Innovation through Creativity and Idea-Sharing:

Promoting innovation within your team involves encouraging creativity and idea-sharing among its members. In this section we explore techniques for stimulating creativity such as brainstorming sessions, hackathons and innovation challenges - emphasizing the importance of creating an environment in which team members feel comfortable expressing their ideas freely while taking risks.

Case Study: Examine a startup known for its innovative culture and analyze their strategies for encouraging creativity and sharing of ideas among team members.

3.2 Ensuring Innovation Resources:

Accessing adequate resources and support for innovation are essential to creating an atmosphere of creativity. In this section we examine the significance of allocating time, budget and tools for experimentation and research as well as real world examples from startups that have successfully created innovation programs, allocated budgets or incubation programs to encourage employee ideas.

Exercise: Develop an innovation program or budget dedicated to experimentation and research at your startup, with guidelines enabling employees to propose innovative projects and execute them successfully.

Conclusion:

In this chapter, we examined strategies for building an effective team and cultivating an environment conducive to innovation within your startup. Through real-life examples, case studies, and exercises we demonstrated the significance of recruiting top talent, creating a collaborative work environment, encouraging creativity and idea-sharing and encouraging creativity and idea sharing between employees. Readers were invited to actively engage in exercises designed to evaluate team dynamics as well as implement innovative practices within their businesses - the next chapter will cover marketing and branding techniques to reach and engage with customers effectively.

Chapter 6: Strategies for Marketing and Branding

Introduction:

Executing effective marketing and branding strategies is the cornerstone of startup success. In this chapter, we explore methods to reach and engage customers effectively, build a powerful brand identity, and implement marketing initiatives that drive growth. By understanding your target market, creating an engaging brand story, and taking strategic marketing measures strategically implemented into place your startup can position itself for ultimate success in a highly competitive landscape.

Section One: Recognizing Your Target Market

Conducting Market Research:

Market research is at the core of successful marketing strategies. In this section we explore its importance, with real world examples showing how startups use research methods such as surveys, focus groups, and data analysis to better understand their target audiences and their needs, preferences and behavior. Real world examples highlight how startups have leveraged market research techniques such as surveys and focus groups in order to identify market trends, target customer segments more precisely, and gain a competitive advantage through this technique.

Exercise: Conduct a market research survey or collect secondary source data in order to gain an insight into your target market and uncover trends and customer preferences. Analyse these results and assess them in terms of customer behavior patterns and preferences.

1.2 Generating Buyer Personas: Buyer personas are fictional representations of your ideal customers that represent demographics, psychographics, and behaviors of their ideal customers. In this section we outline how to create them while considering demographics, psychographics, and behaviors of these customers - this process allows for targeted messaging campaigns, improved customer understanding and successful marketing campaigns! We discuss all these benefits when creating buyer personas in detail.

Exercise: Craft buyer personas for your target audience. Detail their demographics, interests, motivations, pain points and preferred communication channels in these personas to use when creating marketing strategies.

Section 2: Establishing an Engaging Brand Identity

2.1 Crafting Your Brand Story: Establishing an emotional connection with your target audience is vitally important. In this section, we cover the essential elements of a compelling brand story such as mission statement, values statement and unique selling proposition (USP). Furthermore, we examine real world examples of startups with powerful brand stories to examine its effect on market positioning.

Case Study: Examine a startup with an engaging brand story. Investigate how this brand resonates with their target audience, sets them apart from competitors, and influences marketing efforts.

2.2: Establishing a Strong Visual Identity:

An engaging visual identity allows your brand to better express its personality and values, so this section delves into its key components: logos, color palettes, typography and imagery to help create a memorable brand presence that fits with its narrative. We offer advice for creating an integrated and memorable brand story through design elements like this.

Exercise: Create a visual identity for your startup, including logo, color palette and typography elements that reflect its personality while appealing to its target market.

Section 3: Strategic Marketing Initiatives

Content Marketing and Storytelling:
Content marketing can be an invaluable strategy for engaging your target audience and increasing brand credibility. In this section we highlight the significance of creating relevant and valuable content tailored specifically to meet the needs and interests of your target market. Furthermore we explore storytelling techniques for crafting narratives that captivate their attention.

Exercise: Create a content marketing strategy for your startup. Pinpoint key topics, formats, and channels to reach and engage with your target audience effectively.

3.2 Utilizing Digital Marketing Channels: Digital marketing offers many channels for reaching your target audience efficiently. In this section, we explore various digital channels such as Search Engine Optimization (SEO), social media marketing, email marketing and influencer marketing as ways of reaching them effectively - with insights into leveraging these strategies for maximum brand exposure and customer acquisition.

Case Study: Examine a startup which successfully utilized digital marketing channels to expand their customer base, including exploring their strategies, campaign tactics, and impactful impacts on business development.

Conclusion:

In this chapter, we explored marketing and branding strategies for startups. Through real-life examples, case studies, exercises, and discussions we highlighted the importance of understanding your target market, crafting an eye-catching brand identity, and implementing strategic marketing initiatives. Readers were invited to actively participate in these exercises by actively participating in exercises designed to assess marketing needs before devising customized marketing and branding plans tailored specifically for their startups. In Chapter 4, scaling and growth

strategies will be covered so as to take your startup
to new levels of success.

Chapter 7: Scaling and Growth Strategies

Scaling and achieving sustainable growth are important milestones for startups. In this chapter, we explore strategies to successfully expand your customer base while driving continuous expansion. From optimizing operations to exploring new markets or partnerships, we will offer insights on how your startup can position itself for long-term success.

Section 1: Enhancing Operations Optimizations

1.1 Optimizing processes and systems:

Efficiency is crucial to successfully scaling any startup. In this section we cover strategies for streamlining processes, improving productivity, automating repetitive tasks, and streamlining repetitive processes to support rapid expansion. We present examples of successful operations optimization to demonstrate its value.

Case Study: Analyse a startup known for its operational efficiencies. Examine their processes and systems implemented to streamline operations and enable scalability.

As your startup expands, ensuring a scalable infrastructure is in place is of vital importance. In this section, we explore topics like cloud computing, scalable software solutions and flexible IT infrastructure as well as how other startups have built these structures to support growth and meet rising demands.

Exercise: Assess your current infrastructure to identify areas in need of improvement to enhance scalability. Create a plan to create an expandable infrastructure capable of accommodating future growth.

Section 2: Expanding Customer Base

Market Expansion and Diversification:
Entering new markets or targeting different customer segments is a core element of growth strategies, so this section details techniques for market analysis, recognizing opportunities, and formulating entry strategies into new markets. We explore examples of startups who have successfully expanded their customer base through diversification.

Case Study: Assess a startup that successfully expanded their customer base through market diversification. Examine their market analysis process, entry strategies and how this expanded customer base affected growth.

Retaining customers and building networks through referral programs are two effective growth strategies. This section explores customer retention techniques such as personalized experiences, loyalty programs and feedback loops as well as ways to develop referral programs that makes existing customers to refer new ones.

Exercise: For your startup, devise a customer retention strategy by devising strategies to enhance customer experience, foster loyalty and implement referral programs.

Section 3: Partnerships and Collaborations

3.1 Strategic Partnerships:
Building strategic relationships is a great way to speed up startup growth. In this section, we explore their many advantages - access to new markets, shared resources and increased brand exposure among others. Additionally, we provide advice for finding potential partners, forming mutually beneficial relationships and using them for expansion purposes.

Case Study: Examine how one startup achieved substantial growth through strategic partnerships. Investigate their process for finding partners, exchanging value exchanged between parties and the results for their business.

Collaboration with Influencers and Industry Experts:

Working with influencers and industry experts can expand your reach and credibility. In this section, we cover influencer marketing strategies, co-creation content strategies, participating in industry events, as well as real world examples of startups who have successfully collaborated with influencers/industry experts to spur growth.

Exercise: Research influencers or industry experts relevant to your startup's target market and devise a collaboration strategy detailing how you can take advantage of their expertise and networks to drive growth.

Conclusion:

In this chapter, we explored scaling and growth strategies for startups. By using real-life examples, case studies and exercises as examples, we illustrated the importance of optimizing operations, expanding customer bases and forging partnerships in order to foster a culture of growth for your startup. Readers were encouraged to actively participate in exercises as a way of evaluating growth opportunities as well as develop tailored plans to scale them effectively. Finally, Chapter Five will address strategies to sustain success on your entrepreneurial journey over time.

Chapter 8: Sustaining Success and Long-Term Strategies

Introduction:

Sustaining success and implementing long-term strategies are vital to the growth and viability of any startup. In this chapter, we explore strategies that will allow your company to keep momentum, adapt to changing market conditions, foster innovation within your organization, as well as embrace a growth mindset for long-term success.

Section 1 : Continuous Learning and Adaptation

1.1.1: Adopting a Growth Mindset:

A growth mindset provides the basis for continuous learning and adaptation. In this section we discuss its components; emphasizing its benefits of accepting challenges head-on while seeking feedback, persevering despite setbacks, and developing resilience against setbacks. Finally we share real world examples from entrepreneurs who have implemented growth mindset within their organizations.

Exercise: Assess your own mindset and pinpoint areas where embracing a growth mindset might benefit you and your startup. Come up with strategies to overcome challenges, seek feedback and foster a culture of continuous learning in your startup.

1.2 Agile and Adaptive Strategies:

Agility and adaptability are essential in an ever-evolving business landscape, and this section explores agile methodologies, iterative product development processes, and responsive business strategies as ways to stay successful in this fast-changing field. We offer examples of startups who have successfully adopted agile practices so as to remain ahead of competitors.

Case Study: Analyze a startup known for their agile practices and adaptive strategies. Discover how they have welcomed change while iterating products or services and remaining competitive in their industry.

Section 2: Innovation and R&D Initiatives

Fostering Innovation from Within:

Cultivating an atmosphere of innovation is integral to long-term success. In this section we'll look at strategies for encouraging it from within your organization such as idea incubation, cross-functional collaboration and innovation time allocation - real world examples demonstrate how startups have nurtured an innovative mindset among their employees.

Exercise: Introduce an innovation initiative within your startup, such as an idea incubation program or regular innovation workshops, that encourage employees to share innovative ideas that advance the company. This exercise should encourage employees to generate and propose creative concepts to advance the company.

Collaboration to Leverage External Innovation:
Working with external partners such as startups or research institutions can open up a wealth of innovation possibilities. We explore open innovation models, co-creation projects and technology transfer partnerships as a means to uncovering these new avenues of exploration for innovation. Furthermore, we give insights on how startups have successfully used external innovation to expand their product offerings and gain competitive advantages through external innovation partnerships.

Case Study: Examine how one startup has successfully leveraged external innovation. Look into their collaborative partnerships, co-creation initiatives and any effects this had on business growth.

Section 3: Strategic Planning for the Future

3.1 Establishing a Long-term Vision and Roadmap: An accurate long-term vision and strategic roadmap are crucial components to the growth of any startup. In this section we discuss techniques for developing one while setting goals and creating a strategic plan; plus real world examples of companies which successfully aligned their strategies with their long-term visions.

Exercise: Develop and refine a long-term vision and a strategic roadmap for your startup. Outline key milestones, goals, and initiatives that will facilitate its future growth over the next several years.

3.2: Establishing Risk and Resilience:

Risk and resilience management are integral components of long-term success for any startup, and this section covers strategies for identifying, mitigating and building resilience within your startup. We discuss contingency planning, diversification and maintaining strong relationships with key stakeholders.

Exercise: Conduct a risk evaluation and create a risk management plan for your startup business.

Identify potential threats and devise ways to minimize their effect.

Conclusion: In this chapter, we explored strategies for maintaining success and developing long-term strategies in startups. Through real world examples, case studies, exercises, and readers' engagement we highlighted the significance of continuous learning, adaptation, innovation and strategic planning as important aspects of sustaining success on entrepreneurial journeys. Readers were invited to actively engage with these exercises while setting their own long-term goals and developing tailored plans to ensure long-term success on entrepreneurial paths.

Chapter 9: Navigating Challenges and Overcoming Obstacles

Building a startup is no simple journey, with numerous challenges and obstacles in its wake. In this chapter, we outline strategies for navigating common hurdles, surmounting obstacles, and remaining resilient through adversity. By adopting a growth mindset and adopting problem-solving techniques as well as tapping available resources you can overcome any setbacks along your entrepreneurial journey while emerging stronger than before.

Section 1: Assessing Common Startup Challenges

1.1 Exploring the Startup Landscape:

Navigating the startup world can be fraught with difficulties. In this section, we outline common obstacles faced by startups such as funding constraints, market competition, scalability issues and team dynamics issues - along with real world examples of companies that have overcome such hurdles in practice.

Exercise: Assess potential challenges that your startup might face due to industry, market conditions and your business model. Create a plan to effectively address and overcome them.

1.2 Establishing a Growth Mindset:

An essential aspect of successful management, adopting a growth mindset allows individuals and teams to overcome challenges as opportunities for learning and growth. In this section we discuss techniques for cultivating one, such as reframing setbacks as learning experiences, seeking feedback on performance issues and creating a culture of resilience within your startup.

Exercise: Reflect on your current mindset and identify areas where a growth mindset could be fostered. Conceive ways of engaging challenges head-on while learning from setbacks and remaining resilient when facing hurdles.

Section 2: Problem Solving and Decision-Making Strategies

Problem-Solving Frameworks:

Creative problem-solving skills are crucial in your entrepreneurial journey, and this section introduces several frameworks, such as the Plan-Do-Check-Act cycle and 5 Whys technique, that may assist. We present real world examples of startups who have used such frameworks successfully to address challenging problems.

Exercise: Utilizing problem-solving frameworks, apply them to any challenge or obstacle your startup is encountering. Break down the issue, identify potential solutions and devise an action plan to address the situation.

Effective Decision-Making Techniques:

Effective decision-making techniques are key when facing challenges head on, such as SWOT analysis, decision matrices, and risk assessments. We present ways startups have utilized these methods to make well-informed decisions under pressure.

Analyse a startup that faced an enormous decision-making challenge and analyze the steps they used, the tools or frameworks employed, and their outcomes of their decisions.

Section 3: Exploit Resources and Support Networks

Building a Support Network:
An essential aspect of being an entrepreneur is having a reliable support network behind you to offer guidance and provide resources when facing difficult circumstances. In this section we discuss the value of networking, mentorship and joining entrepreneurial communities - as well as providing guidance on identifying mentors or peers who could provide invaluable assistance and advice.

Exercise: Identify key individuals that could form part of your support network, such as mentors, industry experts or fellow entrepreneurs. Create a plan to reach out and foster meaningful relationships.

Entrepreneurs have access to many resources that can assist them in meeting the challenges they face as entrepreneurs, such as government programs, incubators, accelerators, and online communities. We explore these resources here and give insight into how startups have used these tools to overcome hurdles and speed their growth.

Exercise: Do research to identify relevant resources available to startups in your industry or region. Create a plan to utilize these assets effectively so you can address any specific obstacles you encounter along the way.

Conclusion:

In this chapter, we uncovered strategies for successfully navigating challenges and surmounting obstacles during the startup journey. By drawing upon real-life examples, case studies, and exercises we highlighted the significance of adopting a growth mindset mindset while applying problem-solving techniques as well as tapping available resources and support networks to leverage. Readers were invited to actively engage with exercises designed to evaluate personal challenges and devise tailored plans to overcome potential stumbling blocks along their entrepreneurial path.

Chapter 10: Evaluation and Future Improvement

Introduction: For entrepreneurs, reflection and future growth are two integral parts of their entrepreneurial journey. In this chapter, we encourage you to reflect upon your startup journey, evaluate its accomplishments, and plan a course for further growth in future chapters. By celebrating successes while learning from failures and engaging in continuous improvement strategies, you can set the groundwork for a rewarding entrepreneurial future.

Section 1: Recognizing Milestones and Accomplishments

Recollecting Your Startup Journey: Reflecting back on the journey of your startup allows you to acknowledge milestones and achievements along the way, both big and small. We discuss the significance of acknowledging and celebrating every achievement no matter how minor it may seem - insights into how startups have celebrated milestones to boost team morale are also provided here.

Exercise: Create a list of key milestones and accomplishments your startup has accomplished since inception, celebrate these successes with your team, and take note of any significant advancements or setbacks that have occurred along the way.

Failure is an integral part of entrepreneurship, so this section looks at ways failures can be leveraged as opportunities to learn. We share insights on analyzing failures, adapt strategies and iterate on ideas - real world examples show startups who have successfully used failure as an asset for future growth.

Exercise: Recall one failure or setback your startup has experienced and investigate what caused it, extract lessons learned from this instance, and create plans to avoid similar obstacles in future.

Section 2: Innovation and continuous development.

2.1 Establishing a Culture of Continuous Improvement: Continuous improvement is vital for long-term success, so this section explores strategies for building such a culture within your startup. We discuss its advantages such as encouraging feedback, conducting regular evaluations and initiating improvement projects.

Exercise: Implement a continuous improvement program within your startup. Conduct regular evaluation cycles, invite feedback from employees and customers alike, and come up with improvement action plans.

Innovation for Sustainable Growth:

Sustainable growth depends heavily on innovation. In this section we highlight its significance as an enabler for staying ahead of competition and adapting to shifting market dynamics, providing insights on how startups have fostered innovation within their organizations and implemented new ideas to fuel future expansion.

Case Study: Analyze a startup that has successfully adopted innovation for future growth. Consider its strategies, ideation processes and effects of innovation on its business growth.

Section 3: Planning for Future Growth

Evaluation of Opportunities for Expansion:
Assessing opportunities for expansion is integral to future business success, so this section covers techniques for analyzing potential markets, product diversification or geographic expansion. We offer guidance on conducting market research, analyzing feasibility and developing expansion strategies.

Exercise: Explore potential expansion opportunities within your industry or market. Conduct market research, assess feasibility, and create a plan to pursue them.

Setting Strategic Goals for Startup Growth:
Strategic goals provide the basis of any startup's growth trajectory. In this section we discuss the importance of setting SMART (Specific, Measurable, Achievable, Relevant and Time-bound) goals that align with long-term visions, as well as providing insights on how to translate goals into actionable steps and track their progression along the way.

Exercise: Establish one to three year strategic goals for your startup that are SMART and align with its long-term vision. Create action plans and key performance indicators (KPIs) so as to measure progress.

Conclusion: In this chapter, we encouraged you to reflect on your startup journey, recognize achievements, and set a course for future expansion. Through real-life examples, case studies, and exercises we highlighted the importance of continuous improvement, innovation, setting strategic goals, engaging in exercises actively engaging in them to evaluate progress of startup and develop roadmap for its continued development and success.

Conclusion:

For our congratulations are in order! Congratulations on making it through "Startup Secrets Unveiled: A Guide to Launching Your Dream Business." We hope this book has given you valuable insights, practical strategies, and the motivation necessary to undertake your entrepreneurial journey with pride and tenacity.

Through these pages, we have explored the essential elements of starting up a startup, from conceptualization of ideas to scaling your business and planning for long-term success. We have gone into detail regarding market research, funding, team-building, marketing and branding issues as well as challenges encountered and continuous improvement strategies.

Remember, entrepreneurship is an ever-evolving field. The knowledge and tools shared here should serve as a foundation, but ultimately it's up to you to adapt, learn and apply them within the context of your unique startup. Your journey will undoubtedly present unexpected obstacles - embrace them as learning experiences to help drive forward growth and innovation!

Building a successful startup requires hard work, dedication, and the ability to navigate uncertainties and overcome challenges. It's vital to adopt a growth mindset, continuously expand knowledge, and surround yourself with supportive mentors, peers and advisors as part of this journey.

As you journey along your entrepreneurial path, we encourage you to remain curious, take calculated risks and be adaptable. Take advantage of collaboration, learn from both successes and failures alike and welcome feedback and fresh perspectives from others. Even successful entrepreneurs experienced setbacks on their journeys; yet their resilience and determination propelled them forward.

Finally, we wish to express our thanks and appreciation for joining us on this journey. We hope that "Startup Secrets Unveiled" has provided the guidance and inspiration you need to turn your dreams into a reality. Remember: you have the potential to build something amazing, disrupt industries, and leave an enduring legacy.

Armed with knowledge, strategies, and secrets you have uncovered, now is the time to embark upon your entrepreneurial adventure! Accept challenges as opportunities and celebrate victories along the way while always learning and growing - the startup world awaits your unique ideas, passion, and innovation. So, make an impressive statement and make your mark on it all!

Wishing you every success on your entrepreneurial journey.

Ashley Scott